CAST

GUNFIGHTER GLAMOUR

-Painting and diorama by Fidel Rincón
-Conversion of horse and figures by Emilio Arredondo and
 Fernando Andrea

Lt. Col. GEORGE A. CUSTER

-Painting by Raúl G. Latorre

THE CHASE

-Scenery, background, stagecoach and diorama by Baldomero
 Sáiz
-Painting of Indian horses and warriors by Fidel Rincón
-Painting of Indian horse with blanket and rider, and warrior
riding white horse by Luís G. Platón
-Painting of stagecoach figures by J. Francisco Gallardo and
 Jesús Gamarra
-Painting of stagecoach horse team by Mario Ocaña
-Conversion and scratchbuilding by Baldomero Sáiz and
 Fernando Andrea

THE MARSHALL'S OFFICE

-Scenery, electrical work and diorama by Mario & Rafael Milla
-Painting by Fidel Rincón and Mario & Rafael Milla
-Wayne figure painted by Rodrigo H. Chacón and Fidel Rincón

U.S. CAVALRYMAN

-Painting by Jesús Gamarra

EDITED by Andrea Press
TEXT by Raúl G. Nomaldía
PHOTOS by Raúl G. Nomaldía & Acción Press S.A.
DRAWINGS by B. Sáiz, F. Andrea & R. Hernandez
LAYOUT & ART WORK by Raúl G. Nomaldía
TEXT CORRECTION, ENGLISH EDITION by Catherine Mark
PHOTOSETTING by Filma Dos & I.D.A.
PRINTED by Gráficas MAE

Copyright 1997
By Andrea Press
and Andrea Miniatures Division
Internet www.ctv.es\andrea_miniatures

 1

FOREWORD

A number of reasons have induced us to publish the book you now hold in your hands.

Perhaps the first of these reasons is the worldwide Western fashion, particularly widespread in the fifties, that has so much influenced many people now in their forties.

Another, perhaps more important cause, is the tendency that has dominated modelling in recent decades, with virtually nothing but WWII dioramas, vehicles and figures.

Although this has been very positive, by advancing modelling considerably and making it a much more popular hobby, the unlimited panorama of modelling has been ignored by focusing almost exclusively on a particular historical period.

Far from this restricted point of view, however, the number of subjects offered by history and reality goes many times beyond even the possibilities of imagination.

The intention behind this publication is thus to enlarge the present- day perspective of this hobby by presenting some pieces that, due either to the originality of the subject itself or the variation from traditional presentation, represent a real alternative for those modellers and viewers eager to take a further step on the fascinating path of modelling.

Fully aware of the important didactic component that all publications of this sort should incorporate, we have made an effort to show "how the work was done" as clearly as possible by introducing pictures and explanatory drawings whenever it was considered necessary.

I don't want to finish these introductory words without expressing my thanks and admiration to all those artists and craftsmen who contributed so earnestly to make this book possible.

Carlos Andrea

THE GOLDEN WEST

A CAPTIVATING VIEW OF THE WEST THROUGH DIORAMIC MODELLING

INDEX

GUNFIGHTER GLAMOUR
1880

54 mm

No frontier town can be imagined without a series of representative buildings. Like the saloon, the Marshall's office or the bank, the barber shop held a prominent place in the urban setting of western towns. There, cowhands and citizens relaxed in a comfortable seat while the barber performed his art, in a casual atmosphere filled with talk of serious events, anecdotes and local gossip.

Perhaps the most celebrated tonsorial establishment of the West was the Centennial Barber Shop in Dodge City. This gorgeous name has been stolen to adorn the barber shop façade in this diorama featuring two Andrea personalities released years ago, to render the classic topic of a child completely lost in admiration for his greatest idol: the gunfighter...(remember Shane?).

For reasons unknown, some people think that conversion of metal miniatures is more difficult than is the conversion of their resin or plastic counterparts. On the contrary, metal is much more easily converted than resin or plastic, as it can be cut, heated, filed and sandpapered just like the other materials, but bending and shaping are also possible. Finally, and a particular advantage for beginners, paint can be removed easily using standard paint-removers, permitting them to amend possible mistakes.

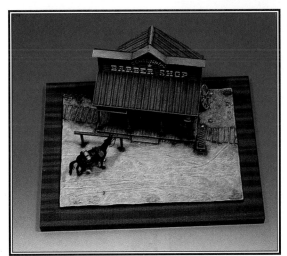

This diorama is a rather simple exercise built around an old Andrea Miniatures kit, made by adding a typical Western building and a horse to balance the composition.

All figures have been converted to some extent before being painted and fixed to the ground.

Despite the belief of some modellers, conversion of stock figures is not difficult once some basic skills are learned.

A key factor in obtaining good results in diorama-making is planning. In this case, before the modelling proper began, a variety of possibilities were tested to achieve maximum dramatic effect in the placement of the elements. The same rules that govern classical painting or drawing apply to the design of a diorama structure: avoid excessive parallelism or symmetry and achieve harmony by judicious distribution of the elements.

The conversion of the Gunfighter consisted in cutting off and turning the head toward the opposite side, fitting him with a new hat from another Andrea figure, and, using a two-component putty, modelling a longer coat, trousers not tucked into the boots, hair and spur straps. The spurs were also taken from another Andrea figure (S4-F7).

The boy's neck was slightly shortened, the head repositioned and a rough wooden revolver added, this last element undoubtedly worn in imitation of his idol.

The little wooden horse was built especially for this diorama. Its construction is fairly simple: the horse and the base can be made by cutting the silhouettes from a wooden sheet or plasticard and the wheels simply modelled from modelling putty. The final touch was added by some lengths of electrical wire to simulate the tail.

One of the most attractive aspects of conversion is to see how a given miniature can change, and even be improved in some cases, by the introduction of variations of diverse complexity.

Through conversion, some modellers achieve results very different from the original stock piece with contributions of great creativity, although it is always possible to build an attractive diorama with no conversion at all.

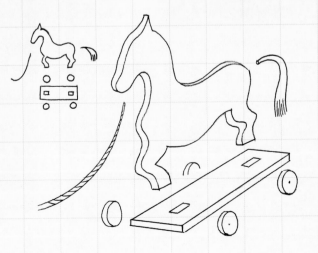

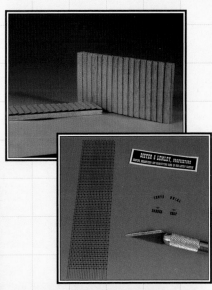

LIST OF ANDREA KITS OR PARTS NEEDED

- S4 A16 Western Facade
- S4 S1 Gunfighter Glamour
- S4 A10 Cowboy Saddle
- S4 A9 Winchester
- S4 S6 (Wheel)
- S5 A17 (Horse's Body)
- S4 F5 (Horse's Neck)
- S4 F1 (Horse's Head)
- S4 F7 (Lariat)
- S4 S3 (Saddle Bag)

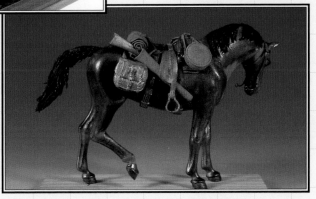

The Western Façade is a high quality product needing no more than a couple of wall sections and a portion of the roof, both made from balsa wood, to add some volume and depth to the building.

The stained glass windows can be made by painting a pattern on transparent plastic sheet or, more simply, by copying the pattern using photosetting devices, a computer or photocopies.

The Gunsfighter's horse was prepared from stock pieces marketed by Andrea Miniatures, with some conversion.   Basically, the horse (S5-A17) was fitted with a new head (from S4-F5) and one of the rear legs raised and repositioned. The rein is made of lead foil and the bit of electrical wire. The tail and horsehair were modelled with Duro putty. The canteen and the carbine holster were modelled with Milliput; unlike Duro, this can be filed and sandpapered, perfect for sealing and levelling joints between pieces.

For most modellers, the painting stage justifies all the others; it is certainly the most appealing aspect of the hobby. Notwithstanding, satisfactory painting can be only achieved when all preparatory stages have been carefully completed. For this reason, all good figures include instructions that should be read with attention.

Figures were painted for many years with oils, which are uncomfortable to handle, toxic and slow-drying, but modern technology now offers water-soluble, fast-drying acrylic paints to the modeller. The Andrea Colour range of acrylic paints, media and varnishes is manufactured to help the demanding modeller in search of absolute pleasure when painting miniatures, without unnecessary, old-fashioned inconveniences.

The technique for using these paints is clean and simple, and consists basically of applying successive layers of very dilute paint to the shape and volumes of the miniature. Each colour is centered on its base colour, or intermediate tone, and highlights and shadows are obtained by mixtures prepared from the base colour. The richness and attractiveness of the figure will depend on the number of gradations applied in the form of colour increases (highlights) and decreases (shadows).

Matching in colour choice and mixing is essential, so that some knowledge of the science of colour is advisable. The colour wheels that can be found in most art shops are very useful for this.

For the beginner, one of the many advantages of metal miniatures over their plastic or resin counterparts is that paint can be removed easily in the case that the result is judged unsatisfactory and a new attempt is desired.

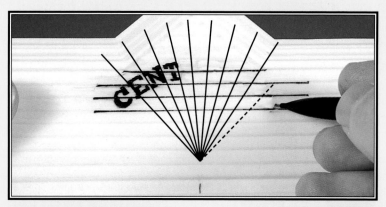

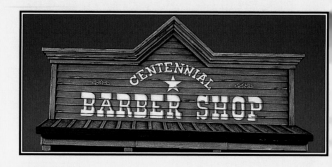

A exacting point is the precise outlining of the lettering on the façade. The Andrea kit includes correctly-scaled lettering that has to be transferred to the façade. There are several ways to do this. The easiest is to cut the lettering provided into strips the width of the wooden battens on the façade and glue them into place. Another solution is to trace the lettering. Here, the letters were drawn with a felt tip pen directly onto the façade, after taking the necessary preliminary measurements and especially the arc section in which the letters are inscribed. Finally, the letters were outlined with paint and brush.

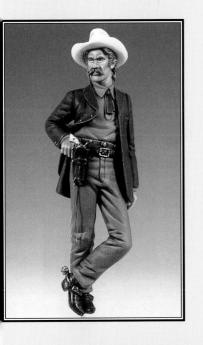

Not many tools are required to paint a figure properly. Perhaps most important after a good, sufficient colour range are the brushes. They should be of maximum quality, with a sharp point and no thinner than number 0. In fact, a set of three of numbers 0, 1 and 2 are sufficient for painting all the miniatures appearing in this chapter.

The colouring of the diverse elements has been chosen carefully to avoid overcolouring and to achieve a balanced effect.

When painting miniatures, it is extremely important to avoid touching the piece at any time. For this, a metal pin is pushed into the piece, then fixed to a small wooden peg to secure the figure during the painting process.

The larger brushes are used for painting horses, as they produce wider areas of dilute colour. In this way, brush strokes applied to a previously-painted surface are invisible.

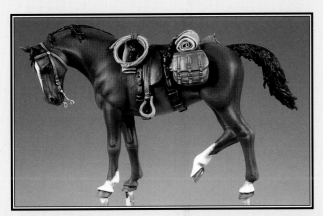

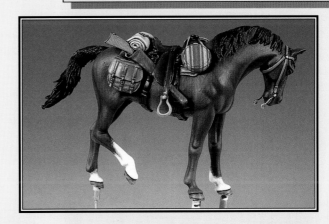

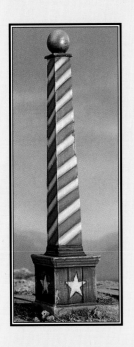

Faces are often one of the most dreaded parts of miniature painting. The series above shows the different stages in painting a face. Care, cleanliness and a bit of practice are required.

One of the most effective techniques in the weathering process is the peeling. The base coat is extended and a coat of masking fluid is then applied to the edges and some protruding areas. Once the masking fluid has set, a new coat of the final colour is applied. When it is completely dry, the masking is erased with a rubber to obtain the peeling effect. This technique was used on the wheel, the barber post and some areas of the façade.

COLOUR CHART FOR GUNFIGHTER AND HORSE

AREA	BASE	HIGHLIGHTING	SHADOWING	NOTES
SKIN	AC-10	AC-10 + (10%) AC-9 (approx. 4 increases)	1st shadow (65%) AC-10 + (35%) AC-16 2nd shadow (25%) AC-10 + (75%) AC-13	Very dilute paint for shadowing.
SHIRT	AC-33	Base + (10%) AC-32 (approx. 4 increases)	AC-33 + (10%) AC-25	
JACKET	(65%) AC-22 + (15%) AC-6 + (20%) AC-26	Base + (10%) AC-20 (approx. 4 increases)	Base + (15%) AC-26	
TROUSERS	(90%) AC-19 + (10%) AC-26	Base + (10%) AC-6 (approx. 4 increases)	Base + (15%) AC-26	Very dilute paint for shadowing.
HAT	(50%) AC-19 + (50%) AC-6	Base + (10%) AC-6 (approx. 4 increases)	Base + (15%) AC-26	
BOOTS & HOLSTER	(75%) AC-26 + (15%) AC-43 + (10%) AC-18	Base + (10%) AC-18 (approx. 4 increases)	Base + (15%) AC-26	AC-43 to satin leather.
REVOLVER	(25%) AC-29 + (75%) AC-27	Base + (10%) AC-29 (approx. 1 increase)		Rounds: Base (50%) AC-27 + (50%) AC-28 Increase: Base + (10%) AC-28
HORSE	(70%) AC-26 + (20%) AC-13 + (10%) AC-43	Base + (10%) AC-18 (approx. 5 increases)	Base + (10%) AC-26	
STOCKINGS	AC-39	Base + AC-6 (approx. 3 increases)		Hooves: Base AC-19 Increase: Base + (10%) AC-6 (approx. 3 increases)
HORSE'S HAIR	AC-26	Base + (10%) AC-19 (approx. 3 increases)		
SADDLE	(80%) AC-13 + (20%) AC-43	Base + (10%) AC-16 (approx. 4 increases)	Base + (15%) AC-17	
SADDLE BAG & CARBINE CASE	(85%) AC-18 + (15%) AC-43	Base + (10%) AC-32 (approx. 4 increases)	Base + (10%) AC-17	
COAT	AC-40	Base + (10%) AC-8 (approx. 4 increases)	Base + (15%) AC-41	String: Base AC-15 Increase: Base + AC-6
CANTEEN	AC-36	Base + (10%) AC-6 (2 increases)		Stripes: AC-20

ALL CODES REFERS TO ANDREA COLOR RANGE

Lt. Col. G. Armstrong Custer
1873

1:8

The legend of the Old West would have been quite different had George Armstrong Custer not existed.

The daring and flamboyant "boy general" of the Civil War became one of the most prominent figures of the West, along with Buffalo Bill, Wild Bill Hickock and Wyatt Earp, even before his famous last stand at the Little Big Horn.

This all-metal bust from Andrea depicts Custer in 1873, three years before he met his terrible end, during the expedition to the Yellowstone. Here he sported his characteristic long hair, although in 1876 he had his hair cut short before leaving for the Little Big Horn.

Raúl García Latorre painted this bust, and has managed an outstanding rendition of Custer's personality. Even his freckled complexion is here, together with the colourful attire of which Custer was so fond.

There is some debate as to whether 1/8 is too large a scale for a bust, as the degree of difficulty varies in direct proportion to size. Though it is obvious that unskilled painting is more apparent at this scale, quality work settles the matter, making it plain that a 1/8 bust clearly enhances first-rate painting.

For the design of this portrait, many photographs of Custer were examined. This was not difficult, as Custer was one of the most frequently photographed men of his era.

This bust is the first in the Andrea 1/8 series, "The Bust Collection". It is cast entirely in metal, which presented a challenge as it is not easy to find such large cast-metal pieces. The figure was designed with only a few hollow parts that fit into each other easily. All joint lines are thus concealed in assembly, making the use of filling paste practically unnecessary.

An original device included in this kit is a small brass corner angle that permits support of the bust from the rear. This gives a pleasant, weightless effect that compensates the always-complicated matter of the harsh cut at the heart in which all busts terminate.

Custer was enchanted by flamboyant garments and was especially fond of the fireman's or sailor's shirts and the fringed buckskins. He had a freckled complexion, well-tanned during the long open-air expeditions, blonde hair and blue eyes.

P ★ A ★ I ★ N ★ T ★ I ★ N ★ G

LIST OF ANDREA KITS OR PARTS NEEDED

- S9 B02 Lt. Col. George A. Custer

Quality tools and materials are essential for a good finish. Andrea Colour paints were applied to the bust using sable brushes, numbers 0, 1 and 2; larger brushes were used for more extensive areas.

A very helpful device is a small commercial medical pill box, used for the colour mixing; it keeps paints moist for a long time before they dry completely. The mixtures dry too quickly on traditional palettes.

COLOUR CHART

* Hat:
Base: (75%) AC-6 + (20%) AC-2 + (5%) AC-1
Lightening: (90%) AC-6 + (10%) AC-2
Shadowing: AC-26

* Skin:
Base: (75%) AC-16 + (5%) AC-2 + (5%) AC-12 + (15%) AC-10
Lightening: (50%) AC-10 + (50%) AC-6
Shadowing: (50%) AC-2 + (50%) AC-12

* Hair:
Base: (10%) AC-26 + (80%) AC-40 + (10%) AC-5
Lightening: (40%) AC-5 + (60%) AC-6
Shadowing: (50%) AC-26 + (50%) AC-40

* Shirt:
Base: (90%) AC-22 + (10%) AC-36
Lightening: AC-20
Shadowing: (85%) Base + (15%) AC-26

* Scarf:
Base: AC-12
Lightening: AC-33
Shadowing: (90%) Base + (10%) AC-3

* Shirt piping:
Base: (50%) AC-19 + (50%) AC-6
Lightening: AC-6

* Coat:
Base: (50%) AC-4 + (10%) AC-1 + (40%) AC-15
Lightening: (80%) AC-6 + (20%) AC-4
Shadowing: (25%) AC-26 + (50%) AC-4 + (25%) AC-2

ALL CODES REFERS TO ANDREA COLOR RANGE

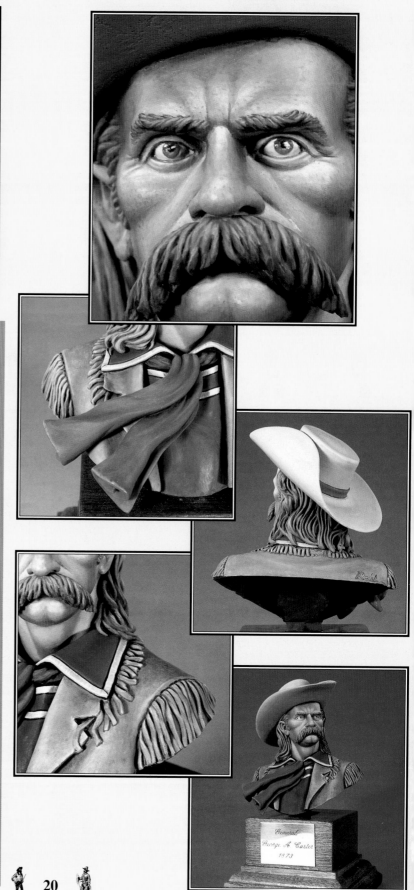

A well-painted face is the most attractive part of a miniature, especially in the case of busts.

The first step in painting the face is to apply the base colour over the entire face area, carefully outlining the already-painted eyes. To achieve the extremely realistic look seen here, highlights and shadows were studied on the bust shape by placing the piece under the overhead light of a lamp.

The face areas receiving more light are the forehead, nose and cheekbones; the maximum light colour — white — was therefore used only on these areas.

The forehead, nose and cheekbones also have intermediate shading areas, as do the chin and the triangle formed by the nose base, the upper lip and the eyelids.

Maximum shadows in dark areas are under the cheekbones, the lower lip and the eyebrow. This last is important and should be painted very carefully, because of its influence on the general balance of the face. Shadow areas were begun just with the base colour and darker shadows prepared using red and dark khaki.

Excess shadowing or lightening should be avoided, as this gives rise to disproportionate contrast or an over-painted effect. Balance between highlights and shadows is essential.

Once the highlighting and shadowing processes are completed, small details such as the freckles can be added.

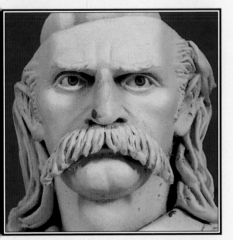

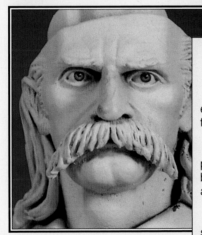

The eyes are a delicate area requiring exquisite care. Eyes and eyebrows are responsible for a large part of facial expresion.

For a realistic effect, the eyeball was painted with a mixture of light grey with a touch of brown as the base colour. Lightening was done by adding white to the lower part of the eyeball.

A little red was added to simulate the small veins in the corners of the eyes.

Another difficult task when painting eyes is to center them properly. Here, two black spots were marked that were then rounded and centered, using successive small strokes until both eyes were perfectly round, centered and of the same size.

For Custer's blue eyes, a reference photograph of a movie star's eyes was used. A mixture of light grey and sky blue was applied to the black circles, until only a thin black line outlined the blue. A "humid" look was effectively represented by painting some highlights on the lower part of the eye and shadowing the upper side. The final touch were some white spots on the pupils and iris. To simulate eyelashes, black was used on the upper eyelid and light brown on the lower lid. To give them a glossy appearance, the eyes were coated with gloss varnish once they were completely painted.

THE CHASE
1880

54 mm

Few things, if any, are more evocative of the Far West than its stagecoaches.

Their romantic image has been the inspiration of many artists, although a large part of their immense popularity may be due John Ford's classic movie, "Stagecoach". This movie also provided the point of departure for the Andrea Miniatures kit that shook the modelling market.

The subsequent release of several galloping Indians makes it possible to build a large-dimensioned diorama recreating one of the most thrilling passages in stagecoach history: the pursuit by a band of Indians — Sioux in this case — determined to capture the coach and its passengers.

Most large-size dioramas do not withstand close-up viewing. In general, when the goal is an overall effect, many subtle details are omitted. This is not the case with "The Chase". Here the figures galloping across the scene have been painted with minute attention to particulars, showing details and motives that can only be appreciated in a closer look and which may even require the help of a magnifying glass. All the passengers are here, with their individual personalities and varied reactions to the attack.

Although they represented a considerable advance in nineteenth century travel facilities, stagecoaches were not comfortable vehicles at all, and must have seemed everything but romantic to the public of the period.

These vehicles evolved from the typical English carriage of the seventeenth century, similar to those used on the first American stagecoach line linking Burlington and Amboy in present-day New Jersey, as long ago as 1732.

23

In 1756, three days and eighteen hours of travel were required to cover a distance that can be done today in an hour and a half.

The first American stagecoach was manufactured by the Abott Downing Company of Concord, New Hampshire in 1827. Their design was so successful that other companies soon imitated it.

Made from wood, iron and leather, the coaches weighed 900 Kg unloaded and were sold for $1,500, a fortune for the period.

It was usual to carry as many as 18 or 20 passengers in and outside the coach, plus the driver and one or two armed guards.

Around the middle of the nineteenth century, a trip from Mississippi to California cost approximately two hundred dollars and lasted, when there were no incidents such as that depicted in the diorama, about three weeks.

Teams of four or six horses were used, depending on the distance to be covered and the terrain. Under normal conditions, a fully-loaded coach might travel at 16 Km/h, though horses had to be changed every 80 to 100 Km for rest and feeding of the passengers.

Despite the hard and often dangerous nature of these voyages, stagecoaches crisscrossed the West for many years. In 1910, the last stagecoaches still serving in remote areas were finally replaced by the recently-developed motor vehicle.

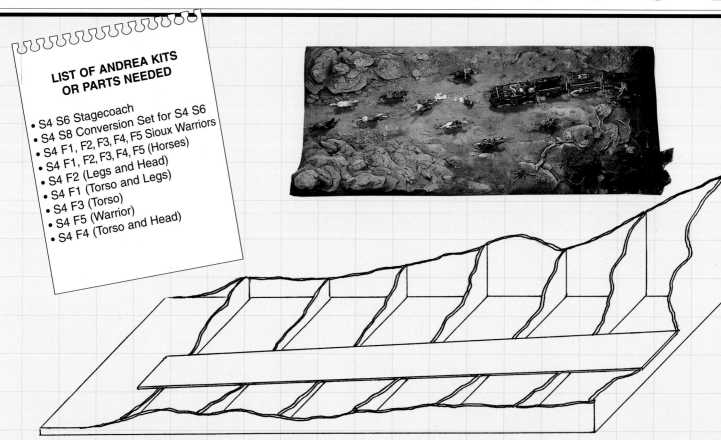

In diorama design, the construction of the ground or scenery on which the figures are to be displayed is a key factor for satisfactory results.

For this diorama, photographs of original landscapes typical of the United States southwest were studied carefully before beginning the modelling.

On a 10 mm-thick board, 5 mm-thick plywood ribs were assembled equidistant from one another and cut down to the ground profile. The next step was to glue narrow strips of paper over the ribs to make a base strong enough to hold the paper maché paste. Once the piece was dry, small natural rocks were added and texturing was done on paper maché paste using spatulas, toothbrushes, etc. Grass was fixed in place with wood glue, as were the smaller rocks and fine sand.

When this was completed, it was time for painting. A first coat of background colour was applied, including browns, greens and greys. The second step was to add some washes with a darker range of the base colours, assuring that crevices and folds were covered.

After drying, extensive dry-brushing with a lighter colour range was applied all over the ground. Finally, some subtle shadowing was airbrushed to outline and delimit some rocks and protuberances.

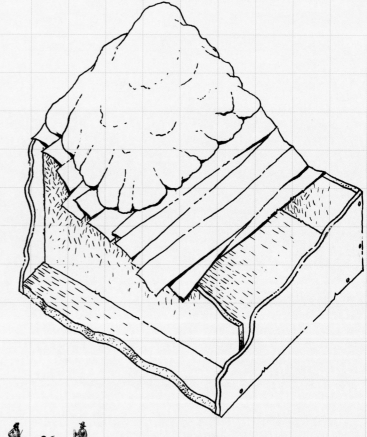

After the process of building and painting the terrain was finished, it was decorated with trees, grass and brush. Elements of vegetation compatible with the rocky, semi-arid ground were chosen, taking care to avoid any excess, which would be impossible in the type of landscape represented here.

The principal trees were prepared by adding some leaves and trunk details to trees used for train dioramas. Small, natural twigs and roots were used to represent fallen and dead vegetation; pebbles give a touch of realism to the banks of the stream and the rocky slopes. Reeds and small shrubs were adapted from decorative elements for train dioramas. The stream is painted on a flat, hard surface. A number of brown, green, and blue tones were used to simulate water, and its flow was suggested by tiny strokes of grey and white. A glossy effect was achieved by applying a coat of vinyl glue and a second of gloss varnish.

27

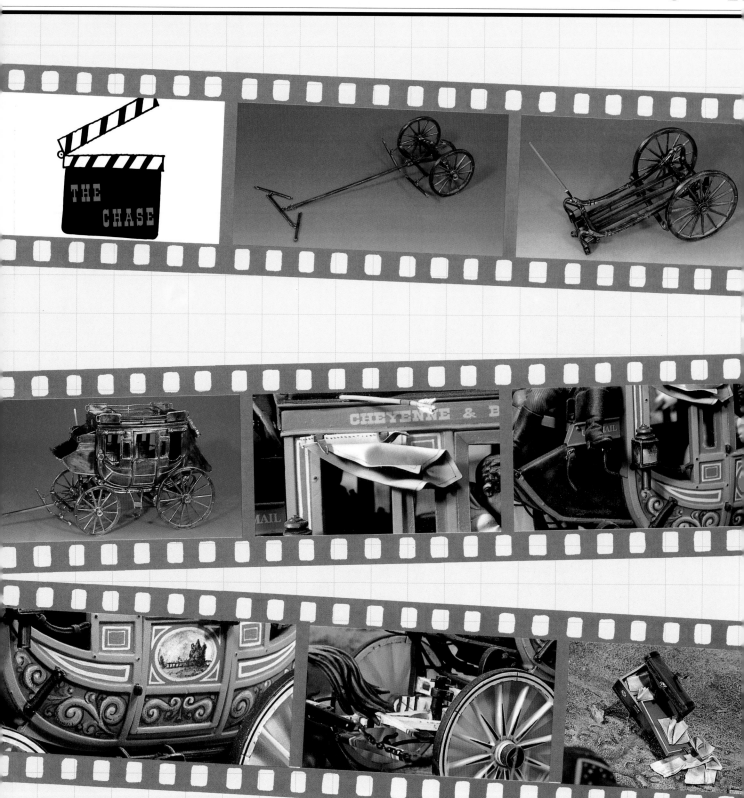

THE CHASE

When assembling the coach, careful attention was paid to the detailed instruction booklet supplied with the kit. It is especially important to check and to "dry run" each step before definitive assembly, and to assure strong joints between those parts that bear the kit's weight. This permits safe transportation and storage of the finished piece.

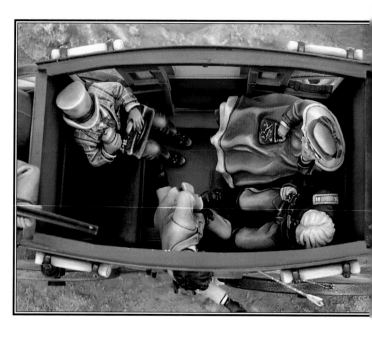

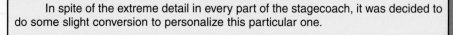

One of the most attractive parts of this Stagecoach kit are its personalities. The 54 mm miniatures are based closely on the characters in the famous movie; even John Wayne is included. All are archetypical of many other Westerns: the gallant cavalry officer, the young, easily-frightened teacher, the gambler and the doctor, abusing his favorite "medicine", even in a moment of maximum danger.

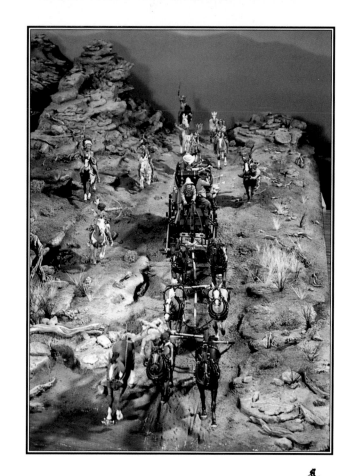

In spite of the extreme detail in every part of the stagecoach, it was decided to do some slight conversion to personalize this particular one.

* A new coachman's seat was designed using lead foil, shaping some creases and adding a small ring and two metal reinforcements to the lower area.

* The lamps were scratchbuilt with strips of plasticard and aluminium. The glass is from transparent plastic cut to measure.

* The curtains were tailored from lead foil, with small buckles added. They were bent to create a sense of motion.

* To enhance the feeling of movement, wheel spokes shadows were airbrushed onto a circular transparent plastic sheet cut to wheel size and fixed to the inner side.

* The luggage hood was scratchbuilt with lead foil and designed a bit loosely, to emphasize motion effects.

* The trunk is made entirely from plasticard and the protruding garments modelled in lead foil and putty.

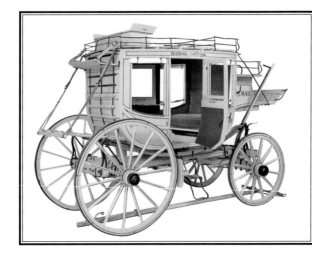

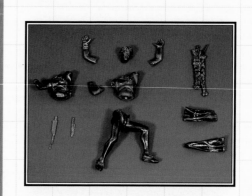

The mounted Indians have been designed with interchangeable torsos, heads, arms, and accessories, giving endless possibilities of creating new figures by simply mixing parts. This is shown with two Indians, the one at the rear of the band and the one that has just shot an arrow. The conversion of the warrior jumping onto the horse team was a bit more difficult than the earlier ones and required more operations.

His mouth was opened to insert the knife, which was fashioned using lead foil for the blade and two plastic strips for the handle. The torso is from kit S4-F04; its right arm was cut at armlet level using a very thin metal saw. Legs and arms come from kit S4-F05. The assembly bolts were erased on all parts to permit fine adjustment; a new bolt was made with a small steel pin inserted into the right foot to fix the figure securely to the horse. The bow case strap was made of lead foil and the loincloth (S4-F04) was bent slighly to increase realism. The armlet was erased with the help of a craft blade and a file.

To assemble the parts forming the body, the union areas were drilled with a 2 mm bit and the holes filled with a two-component paste. Steel pins (made from steel paper clips) were then inserted to permit the joining of the parts in a natural manner.

Once the pieces were correctly positioned and the paste had set, the gaps between pieces were filled.

The antiquity of the subject, the few surviving stagecoaches and the inexistence of colour photography at the end of the past century make it impossible to list a complete choice of colours for painting the stagecoach. The red-yellow combination used in the diorama was typical enough and may even have been the most common.

There are stagecoaches painted in yellow and green, and other colours should be not ignored. Common to all were the scroll and filigree work so typical of Victorian fashion, of which a wide diversity existed.

Another very common ornament was the painting of landscapes on coach doors.

Although the Andrea Miniatures kit includes superb dry transfers for decoration, some were discarded in favour of beautifully hand-painted detailing. Similar motives can be found in specialized publications, movie still shots, or museums.

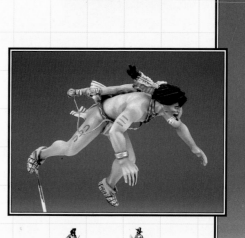

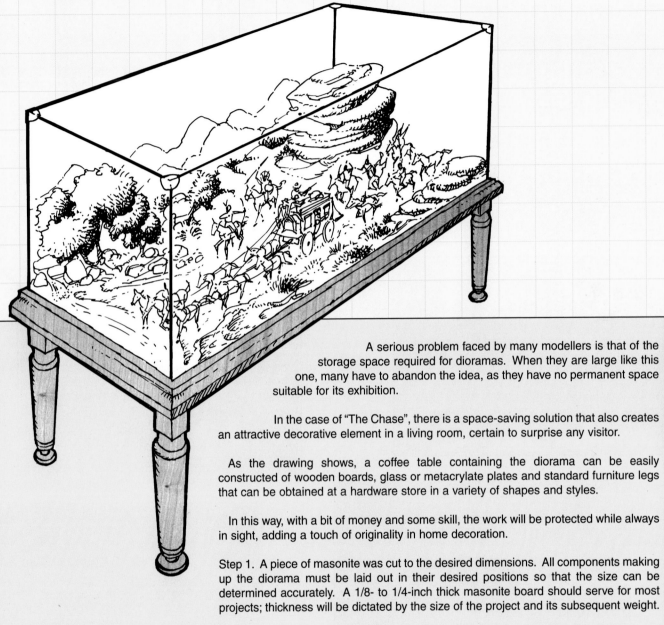

A serious problem faced by many modellers is that of the storage space required for dioramas. When they are large like this one, many have to abandon the idea, as they have no permanent space suitable for its exhibition.

In the case of "The Chase", there is a space-saving solution that also creates an attractive decorative element in a living room, certain to surprise any visitor.

As the drawing shows, a coffee table containing the diorama can be easily constructed of wooden boards, glass or metacrylate plates and standard furniture legs that can be obtained at a hardware store in a variety of shapes and styles.

In this way, with a bit of money and some skill, the work will be protected while always in sight, adding a touch of originality in home decoration.

Step 1. A piece of masonite was cut to the desired dimensions. All components making up the diorama must be laid out in their desired positions so that the size can be determined accurately. A 1/8- to 1/4-inch thick masonite board should serve for most projects; thickness will be dictated by the size of the project and its subsequent weight.

Step 2. With the masonite cut to size, a wooden frame was constructed to fit around it. Before the frame was glued together, a groove was routed into each section so that a glass cover could be fitted later. When the glued frame had dried completely, the masonite base was fitted and glued into place.

Step 3. To give the table its desired height, legs were purchased at a hardware store. Once again, leg size depends on the size of the display being built. These legs can be purchased either finished or unfinished, depending on the builder's preferences.

Step 4. Metal brackets were fastened to the bottom corners of the framework assembly. These brackets are often provided with the legs. When the brackets were securely positioned, all legs were screwed on.

Step 5. The final item needed for the table was the glass case. One solution is to take the completed table to a glass company to have the top constructed. Glass was chosen rather than Plexiglas or acrylic because it does not cloud up or show scratches quite as noticeably.

A six-horse team has been built. The choice of horse colours is thus of foremost importance, as an improper selection from the wide variety of possibilities could give an unreal effect or lack of colour harmony.

Specialized books were consulted to check the authenticity of colours and marking features.

The whole of the harness parts, formed of excellent photoetchings, flexible metal parts and brass rings, allows the rendering of a surprisingly accurate miniature, as can be appreciated in the photographs.

The harnesses are separate parts that fit onto the bare horses, allowing the testing of different horse positions to give maximum visual effect.

Tails and manes are also interchangeable, increasing assembly choices.

The harness has been painted in black leather to match the rest of the leather elements of the coach. The realistic effect that can be achieved with this horse team is surprising because of the sensation of motion and the sharp detail of the many parts.

The mustangs have been decorated with feathers fixed to their tails, manes, and even to the long reins.

Feathers were assembled by tying with fine electrical wire or by drilling the piece to introduce the feather. Reins were made by the classical method of twisting together three lengths of electrical wire. For war painting, a huge range of motives was used, all of a symbolic nature. Many represented the warrior's bravery or his gods, which were used as talismans.

The horses have been painted to offer a wide variety of the most usual symbols sported by the Indian warriors.

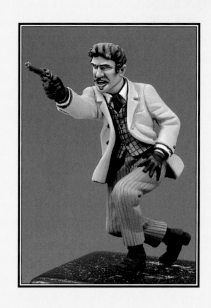

P ★ A ★ I ★ N ★ T ★ I ★ N ★ G

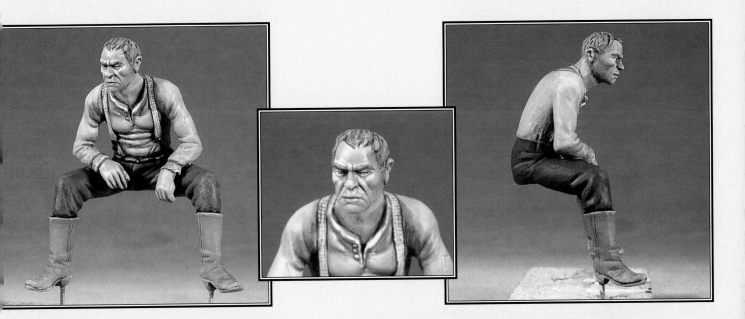

The prisoner was made by converting Andrea figure SG-A1, whose boots were replaced by those from another Andrea figure (S4-F6). The trousers, the shirt and suspenders were remodeled with a two-component paste. The head was from Andrea kit S4-F8, for which the skull was completed and some facial redetailing added.

Both the light skin tone and the creamy colour of the undershirt are considered to enhance this figure, who is displayed in a softly-lighted area of the diorama.

The original colours of the wood used in the wainscoating and the floor have been left unchanged, adding only some veins with light tones and others darker, all with very thin brush strokes.

For the brick walls, the base colour was dark grey, to which some dry brushing was added, enlightening with reddish tones.

Once a balanced tone had been obtained, random bricks were painted with slightly different tones; the lighter with orangish colours (AC-32) and the darker in blackish tones. More dry-brushing was added with greenish strokes, followed by some very dilute washing. The final touches were some airbrush shadowing on the corners and edges with very dilute black paint.

The window bars were airbrushed with "gun-metal" paint, shadowed with black washes and weathered by thin brush strokes to simulate peeling and other markings.

  59

U.S. CAVALRYMAN
1876

90 mm

The traditional 90 mm size represents a beautiful balance between detail and size within the wonderful history of metal miniatures. Many artists consider 90 mm figures as the maximum size for a miniature, followed by statuettes, which are not considered proper miniatures.

The miniature depicts one of the most widespread topics of the West: the flamboyant Cavalry officer (probably of the Seventh) with his fireman's shirt and the fringed jacket that George Custer popularized so successfully.

All the U.S. Cavalry paraphernalia is realistically represented here by the expert hands of Jesús Ara, who designed the figure inspired by a work of the famous Western artist Ron Tunison, to whom this miniature is a kind of tribute.

Life in the frontier army post was quite different from that which Hollywood has taught us: low salaries, long working days at the stables, much drilling and boredom were the staple of the U.S. Cavalry soldier's life at this time. Only a few finished their years of service with some experience in engagements with Indians. As can be expected, the situation was not the same for the officers, who could mitigate this rather coarse life with social parties, sports and, in many cases, spirited drinks.

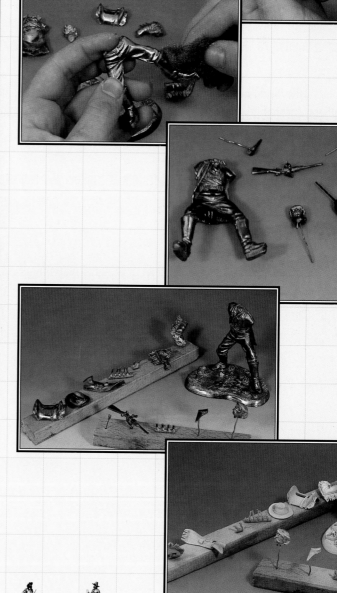

Goods tools and equipment are essential for quality work.

This figure was prepared using a couple of small files, waterproof sandapaper, some fine drills, wires or paper clips to reinforce the joints between parts, Milliput filling paste to seal joints and correct possible flaws, cyanocrylate and two-component glues and a hobby craft blade with a handle to hold the drills.

Once ready for work, the first step was to prepare and clean all metal parts, eliminating mould lines, sprue, flaws and any imperfection that might be present using the hobby craft blade, files and finally, sandpaper. All these tools are to be used with care and attention to avoid damaging any details.

To avoid touching the figure while painting, a simple and effective solution is to drill holes into the parts to receive steel "pins", thus procuring a strong joint. Drills of 0.5, 1 and 2 mm were used, depending on the size of the part and of the figure.

Polishing and washing assured good paint coverage, both in priming and in colour application steps.For polishing, it is best to use a mini-drill with nylon or brass heads, never steel. Subsequently, all parts were washed with soap and water to eliminate casting lubricants, using a tooth brush or similar. The piece was dried with lint-free cloths or a hairdryer.

Priming was done with light colours such as white or grey. It can be applied with a brush, airbrush or by mean of sprays, available in most model shops.

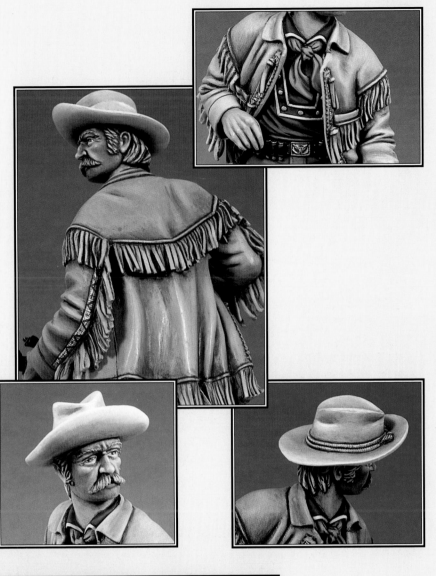

COLOUR CHART

*Hat
  Base: (50%) AC-6 + (45%) AC-19 + (5%) AC-39
  Lightening: AC-6
  Shadowing:(50%) Base + (25%) AC-26 + (25%) AC-42

*Hat cording
  Base: (50%) AC-40 + (50%) AC-8
  Lightening: AC-7
  Shadowing: (50%) AC-40 + (25%) AC-26 + (25%) AC-42

*Buckskins
  Base: (50%) AC-40 + (50%) AC-6
  Lightening: AC-6
  Shadowing: Washes with (50%) AC-40 + (50%) AC-17
  and AC-26

*Bandanna
  Base: AC-12
  Lightening: (50%) AC-33 + (50%) AC-32
  Shadowing: AC-27

*Boots and belt
  Base: AC-27
  Lightening : (50%) AC-18 + (50%) AC-33
  Shadowing: AC-27

*Belt buckle
  Rich gold (alcohol paint)

*Trousers
  Base: AC-22
  Lightening: AC-20
  Shadowing: (50%) AC-22 + (50%) AC-26

*Shirt
  Base: AC-22
  Lightening: AC-20
  Shadowing : (50%) AC-22 + (50%) AC-26

*Saddle
  Base: (50%) AC-17 + (50%) AC-33
  Lightening: AC-33
  Shadowing : (50%) Base + (50%) AC-26

*Flesh
  Base: (50%) AC-41 + (50%) AC-15
  Lightening: (75%) AC-6 + (25%) AC-43
  Shadowing : AC-41 + AC-15 + AC-26

*Beard
  Base flesh mixture + AC-26

*Carbine
  Metal parts:
  Base: (75%) AC-27 + (25%) AC-29
  Lightening : AC-29
  Shadowing: AC-27
  Wood:
  Base: AC-41 with washes of AC-17 and AC-26
  Lightening: AC-15
  Indian decorations: They were painted on a white
  base colour (AC-6), then drawing in the chosen colour.
  Very fine lines were drawn to shape small squares
  using black (AC-26).

*Grass
  Base: AC-38
  Lightening: AC-8
  Shadowing: (50%) Base + (50%) AC-26

*Terrain
  Base: AC-40
  Lightening: AC-6
  Shadowing: (50%) Base + (50%) AC-41

ALL CODES REFERS TO ANDREA COLOR RANGE

MORE AVAILABLE KITS IN SERIES IV " THE GOLDEN WEST "

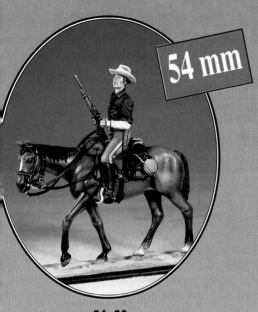

54 mm

54 mm

WHITE METAL CASTINGS

S4 S3
U.S. CAVALRYMAN ON THE TRAIL (1880)

S4 F8
THE SHOOTIST

54 mm

S4 S5
CUSTER´S LAST STAND

90 mm

54 mm

AVAILABLE WORLDWIDE
FROM
SPECIALIST MODEL SHOPS

S8 F11
MOUNTAIN MAN (1860)

S4 A16
WESTERN FACADE

MORE AVAILABLE KITS IN SERIES IV " THE GOLDEN WEST "

54 mm

54 mm

**WHITE METAL
CASTINGS**

**S4 S7
SHOT DOWN**

**S4 F7
COWBOY**

90 mm

54 mm

**S4 F9
WYATT EARP**

**S8 F3
CRAZY HORSE (1876)**

54 mm

**AVAILABLE WORLDWIDE
FROM
SPECIALIST MODEL SHOPS**

**S4 S4
THE RIVER MARAUDERS (1750)**

 66

ANDREA COLOR

 AC-1 FIELD GRAY / UNIFORME ALEMAN

 AC-2 ENGLISH KHAKI / UNIFORME INGLES

 AC-3 OLIVE GREEN / UNIFORME AMERICANO

 AC-4 JAPANESE KHAKI / UNIFORME JAPONES

 AC-5 RUSSIAN KHAKI / UNIFORME RUSO

 AC-6 FLAT WHITE / BLANCO MATE

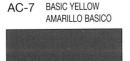 AC-7 BASIC YELLOW / AMARILLO BASICO

 AC-8 GOLDEN YELLOW / AMARILLO DORADO

 AC-9 LIGHT FLESH / CARNE CLARA

 AC-10 DARK FLESH / CARNE OSCURA

 AC-11 MAGENTA / MAGENTA

 AC-12 BASIC RED / ROJO BASICO

 AC-13 DARK RED / ROJO OSCURO

 AC-14 PURPLE / PURPURA

 AC-15 OCHRE / OCRE

 AC-16 MEDIUM BROWN / MARRON MEDIO

 AC-17 DARK BROWN / MARRON OSCURO

 AC-18 REDDISH BROWN / MARRON ROJIZO

 AC-19 MEDIUM GREY / GRIS MEDIO

 AC-20 LIGHT BLUE / AZUL CLARO

 AC-21 BASIC BLUE / AZUL BASICO

 AC-22 PRUSSIAN BLUE / AZUL PRUSIA

 AC-23 VIOLET / VIOLETA

 AC-24 LIGHT GREEN / VERDE CLARO

 AC-25 DARK GREEN / VERDE OSCURO

 AC-26 FLAT BLACK / NEGRO MATE

 AC-27 GLOSS BLACK / NEGRO BRILLO

 AC-28 GOLD / ORO

 AC-29 SILVER / PLATA

 AC-30 COPPER / COBRE

 AC-31 BRONZE / BRONCE

 AC-32 FRENCH ORANGE / NARANJA FRANCES

 AC-33 NAPOLEONIC RED / ROJO NAPOLEONICO

 AC-34 NAPOLEONIC BLUE / AZUL NAPOLEONICO

 AC-35 MEDITERRANEAN BLUE / AZUL MEDITERRANEO

AC-36 BALTIC BLUE / AZUL BALTICO

AC-37 EMERALD GREEN / VERDE ESMERALDA

AC-38 NAPOLEONIC GREEN / VERDE NAPOLEONICO

AC-39 BEIGE / BEIGE

AC-40 EARTH / TIERRA

AC-41 WOOD / MADERA

AC-42 BROWN LEATHER / MARRON CUERO

AC-43 GLOSS MEDIUM / MEDIUM BRILLANTE

AC-44 MAT VARNISH / BARNIZ MATE

AC-45 GLOSS VARNISH / BARNIZ BRILLO

* **Great coverage.** Best covering acrylics in a 17 ml. squeeze jar. This great advantage saves time, money and improves painting quality. Second coats are not needed.

* **Compact colour selection.** You don't need to buy a lot of jars to achieve good results in the painting of figures. A carefully - selected range of 45 colours, including specific uniform colours.

* **Highly pigmented.** More pigment means better blending, colour mixing and richer - looking colours.

* **Super brushing consistency.** Rich and creamy for smooth and easy brush strokes.

* **Long shelf life.** Bottled ANDREA COLOR paints will last for years and years without getting stringy, lumpy or hard.

* **Air brushing.** because of ANDREA COLOR'S unique formulation, the paints can be thinned with water to the consistency of milk for air brushing.

* **Primary colours.** A full line of primary colours is included so that artists can mix and tone a complete line of choice. These colours are called BASIC RED, BASIC BLUE and BASIC YELLOW.

After years of trial and research with many different paints, we have finally come to a compact, but complete line of acrylic paint which, due to their exceptional characteristics, offer unbeatable performance.

Commercialized by: ANDREA S.L. Maestro Zudaire, s/nº. Los Negrales. Villalba. 28049 Madrid. Spain